A New True Book

CONSERVATION

By Richard Gates

*This "true book" was prepared
under the direction of
Illa Podendorf,
formerly with the Laboratory School,
University of Chicago*

CHILDRENS PRESS, CHICAGO

Natural water fountain,
Grinell Glacier, Montana

PHOTO CREDITS

Jerry Hennen—2, 11 (middle & bottom left), 29 (bottom), 40 (right), 42 (2 photos)

James P. Rowan—Cover, 4, 23

Bill Thomas—44 (2 photos)

Reinhard Brucker—6, 27 (right)

Joseph A. DiChello, Jr.—35

Lynn M. Stone—7, 8, 13, 31 (2 photos), 38 (2 photos), 39, 40 (left), 41

Julie O'Neil—11 (top left)

Allan Roberts—11 (top & bottom right), 12, 20, 34

United States Department of Agriculture, USDA—14, 17, 19, 24, 27 (left)

Judy Potzler—29 (top)

James M. Mejuto—32, 37

COVER—Long's Peak, Rocky Mountain National Park

Library of Congress Cataloging in Publication Data

Gates, Richard.
  Conservation.

  (A New true book)
  Revised edition of: The true book of conservation. 1959.
  Summary: Explains how people have disrupted ecological chains, and what should be done now to protect our natural resources.
    1. Conservation of natural resouces—Juvenile literature. [1. Conservation of natural resources] I. Title.
  S940.G37   1982   333.7'2   81-38482
  ISBN 0-516-01618-0   AACR2

TABLE OF CONTENTS

Glacier National Park

THE LAND IS RICH

At one time, forests covered more than half of North America.

Trees stood close together. A squirrel could travel in them for many miles and not touch the ground.

Buffalo, Wind Cave National Park

Buffalo herds roamed through tall grass. They drank at the clear, cool streams.

There were many passenger pigeons. Sometimes a flock of them was so large it made the sky look dark.

Many whooping cranes lived in the marshes.

Many beautiful wild flowers helped to make the soil rich.

Whooping crane, an endangered bird

Elk, Yellowstone National Park

HOW THE LAND WORKED

This land had grass, forests, streams, animals, and wild flowers. Each depended on the other in some way.

Forests help grasslands. Forests keep streams from running wild and washing soil away.

Broad leaves catch the rain. Deep roots help hold the rain.

Forests help to clear the air and make the soil good. They help to keep the winter air from getting too cold, and the summer air from getting too hot.

Forests shade the wild flowers. They shelter the little animals and give birds a home.

Squirrels scatter seeds from trees. The seeds grow into other trees.

Top left: Red fox
Middle left:Green frog next to pitcher
plant
Bottom left: Red trillium
Top right: Chipmunk
Bottom right: Male cardinal

Beavers enter their lodge through an underwater tunnel.

Beavers build dams.
These help to keep the
water from rushing off.
Rushing water can take
good soil with it.

Birds eat insects that harm the trees.

Even the smallest lady's slipper adds beauty and color to the land. When it dies, it gives something back to the soil.

Lady's slipper

Wagon trains carried settlers west.

PEOPLE COME
TO THE LAND

This land community of plants and animals was not upset when few people lived in it.

But more and more people came. People must have food and homes.

Farmers used big plows. They cut into grass and sod that had not been plowed before. They cut down forests for wood. They burned trees to clear the land for crops.

Small animals and birds had to look for new homes.

Farmers used plows and horses to clear the land.

THE LAND IS HURT

As years went by, more things happened to the land.

Rain had once dripped from leaves and branches and through the thick grass. It had soaked slowly into the ground.

Now the rainwater began to rush through plowed fields. There was no grass

Years of over-working this land left it severely damaged.

to hold it. The rain hurried
over land where forests
once had been. As the
water ran, it took good soil
with it.

The east and west forks of the Whitewater River meet in
Indiana. You can see how the east fork (right) is polluted with silt
from a nearby gravel pit.

The water ran into the streams. The clear streams became muddy with soil. The extra water broke off the grass on the stream banks. Whole chunks of the banks floated away.

Farm land that once had been rich became poor from overuse. Crops could no longer grow there. Animals could not find grass to eat. When this happened, the people would move to new land. There was plenty of land.

Prairie homestead, Kadoka, South Dakota

Before laws protecting animals, hunters could kill as many animals as they wanted.

ANIMALS DISAPPEAR

Railroads were built. More people came. They built small towns. The small towns grew into great cities. There were fewer places for wildlife to live in peace.

Flocks of passenger pigeons were shot or trapped and shipped to market. Now there is not one passenger pigeon left.

The great herds of buffalo almost disappeared. Now there are only a few whooping cranes left.

Above: Theodore Roosevelt's cabin in Medora, North Dakota

Left: President Theodore Roosevelt loved the outdoor life and believed conservation was needed to protect wildlife and natural resources for the future.

SAVE THE LAND

In the early 1900s, some wise people began to think about the land. "People are members of this land community," they thought. "We must respect the other members. We must learn to use the land and the forests well. We must understand the birds and the animals and the wild flowers. We must speak up for their right to live."

Guarding what we have, and not wasting it, is called conservation.

Conservation is a wonderful thing for our land.

Swamp Lake near Shoshone National Forest

Mountain goat in Glacier National Park

It is as close to home as your own backyard.

It is enjoying a tree without pulling off leaves or breaking branches. It is guarding a robin's nest so the eggs can hatch. It is letting ladybugs go in peace so they can eat harmful insects on plants. It is letting a frog stay in its home. It is letting wild flowers grow undisturbed.

Boy watching a caterpillar

Robin with young

Tree planting

CONSERVATION WORKERS

There are many people who work for conservation. Forest conservation workers plant new trees when old ones are cut down. They protect young trees from little animals. They spot and cure disease in trees. They try to control harmful insects.

This helicopter is returning from dumping chemicals on a forest fire in Wyoming's Medicine Bow National Forest.

Forest workers do all they can to prevent forest fires. When a fire breaks out, they spot it quickly. They work to control it and put it out quickly.

Soil conservation workers
help farmers keep their
land safe and rich.

Rushing water is made to slow down. Water runs down slopes. So farmers plow across the slopes. More water and soil stay on the hills this way.

Streams are also dammed. Trees are planted. Thin grass is helped to grow thicker. Sometimes grassland is protected by fences.

Theodore Roosevelt Lake in Arizona

Animals cannot eat the
grass. The grassland then
has time to heal and grow.
Fast-growing grass is also
planted in ditches. The
grass roots help hold the
soil.

Special plowing, trees, and grass help keep the soil in place.

Wildlife conservation workers help the birds, animals, and fish of our country to live.

The barn owl (left) and the Florida panther (right) are endangered animals.

Conservation workers "web-tag" goslings.

First they study the
animals and their homes.
They make sure people
obey the laws. They
protect animals and birds
against hunters who do not
obey laws.

Above: Student conservation group tests
creek water in Illinois.
Left: Teacher and a high school student work
with sea turtle conservation in Florida.

They help raise fish.
Then they put the fish into
lakes and streams. Care is
being taken to keep water
pure.

Soybeans grow on what was once a tall grass prairie in Illinois.

WHY WE PROTECT
THE LAND

We need good land to give us food.

Minerals from the land must be used well and without waste.

National Elk Refuge, Jackson Hole, Wyoming

Logan Pass, Glacier National Park

Wildlife and wild flowers
must be protected. They
do not just add beauty to
the land. They are
important in more ways
than we know.

Top: Baxter State
Park, Maine
Bottom: Olympic
National Park

44

Conservation means keeping all of our land beautiful and healthy.

Our land community is kept safe in state and national parks. Here, and in other wilderness areas, we can feel the wonder of our land and its wildlife.

WORDS YOU SHOULD KNOW

bank—the sloping ground at the edge of a river or lake

broadleaf(BRAWD • leef)—a leaf that is wide

community(kuh • MYOON • itee)—an area where living things live together

crops(KROPZ)—plants grown for food

dependent(dih • PEN • dint)—relied on

disturb(diss • TERB)—to upset or change

ditch—long, narrow hole dug in the ground

enforce(en • FORSS)—to make sure a rule or law is obeyed

flock—a group of animals that live together

forest—a place where many trees grow close together; woods

furrow(FER • oh)—a long, narrow cut made in the ground

gully(GUL • ee)—a ditch cut in the earth by running water

herd—a group of animals that live together

manage(MAN • ije)—to control; run

marsh—an area of low, wet land; swamp

mineral(MIN • er • il)—a useful material that is found in the earth

plow—a farm tool used for breaking up soil

reckless(REK • less)—careless

respect(ree • SPEKT)—regard; hold in honor

restock(REE • stahk)—put more of something in; to fill again

roam(ROME)—to travel; wander

shelter(SHELL • ter)—a place of protection; safe place

sod(SAHD)—grass and soil held together tightly

topsoil(TOP • soyl)—the rich layer of soil at the surface of the ground

trickle(TRIK • il)—to flow drop by drop

undisturbed(UN • diss • TERBED)—not to change; calm

whooping crane(WOOP • ing • CRAIN)—a large bird with long legs and black and white feathers

INDEX

About the author

Richard Gates is a professional artist who lives and works in Michigan. His love of the beauty of our land led to his interest in conservation and to this book which instills in young minds a new appreciation of and responsibility for the natural beauties and resources of our land.

SS18 SANDY SPRINGS

Gates, Richard.
  Conservation / by Richard Gates. --
Chicago : Childrens Press, c1982.
  45 p. : chiefly col. ill. ; 22 cm. --
(A New true book)
  Previously published as: The true
book of conservation. 1959.
  Summary: Explains how people have
disrupted ecological chains, and what
should be done now to protect our
natural resources.
  ISBN 0-516-01618-0

1. Conservation of natural resources
--Juvenile literature. I. Title